TRADING STRATEGIES

Top 3 Profitable

Trading Strategies and Practical Techniques

Abraham Robert. C

Copyright©2024 Abraham Robert .C

All Rights Reserved

Bonus package

Free video access

This book comes with a link that grants you unique access to a complimentary video version, which will enhance your reading experience by adding a visual learning element.

TABLE OF CONTENT

Chapter 1 _____ **8**

Trading strategy _____ **8**

    Benefits of using a trading strategy _____ 11

    Overview of the top best three profitable trading strategies _____ 12

        Trend Trading _____ 12

        Breakout Trading _____ 16

        Range Trading _____ 18

Chapter 2 _____ **20**

Strategy 1: (Trend trading strategy) _____ **20**

    Identifying a trend _____ 21

    Important principle and component of trend trading strategy _____ 27

        Trend Confirmation _____ 27

        Entry and Exit Points _____ 28

        Risk Management _____ 29

        Patience and Discipline _____ 29

        Trade management _____ 30

        Adaptability _____ 30

Avoid overtrading. _____ 31

Continuous Learning _____ 31

Type of Trend Following Strategies _____ 32

Short-term Trend Following Strategy _____ 32

Intraday Trend Trading _____ 33

Long-term trend following strategy _____ 34

Position trading _____ 34

Popular trend trading indicators _____ 35

Moving Average Convergence Divergence (MACD) _____ 35

The Relative Strength Index (RSI) _____ 35

Parabolic SAR _____ 36

Chapter 3 _____ *38*

Strategy 2: (Breakout trading strategy) _____ 38

Breakout in Trading _____ 38

_____ 39

Support _____ 39

Resistance _____ 41

Types of Breakout Strategy _____ 43

Continuation Breakout Strategy _____ 43

Reversal Breakout Strategy _____ 47

How to Spot a Reversal Breakout Strategy _____ 48

False Breakouts _____ 53

How to Trade a False Breakout _____ 55

Chapter 4 _____ 60

Strategy 3: (Range or a sideways trading strategy) _____ 60

Identifying a Range or Sideways Market _____ 62

How do you know when a range or sideways market will end _____ 63

Advantages of trading a range or sideways market _____ 64

Limitations of trading a range or sideways market _____ 66

Chapter 5 _____ 68

Conclusion _____ 68

Time frame _____ 68

Position size _____ 69

Create a sound trading plan _____ 70

Practice with a demo account _____ 71

Choose the Right Broker _____ 72

Continuously educate yourself _____ 73

Chapter 1

Trading strategy

Trading strategies are systematic methods for buying and selling assets in financial markets. They are based on a predetermined set of guidelines that assist define the appropriate time to enter or quit a position.

Most techniques use technical or fundamental analysis to discover opportunities in financial markets and give a strong basis for trading decisions.

Technical analysis forecasts future prices based on previous price activity, whereas fundamental analysis examines how economic, political, and social issues influence price movements.

Traders might choose to use a single strategy or combine several methods to suit their individual trading style and aims. Finding the appropriate trading technique usually takes testing and modifying, and traders must constantly adapt their strategies.

What's the distinction between trading strategy and trading style?

Although there is a lot of confusion between trading strategy and trading style, there are certain key distinctions that every trader should understand. A strategy is a highly specific methodology for determining the price points at which one should enter and exit a trade, whereas a trading style delineates a comprehensive approach to determining the frequency and duration of open positions.

Benefits of using a trading strategy

There are limitless chances in financial markets, and trading techniques assist traders in navigating them and detecting potential faster.

Having a strategy allows you to make better judgments and optimize the outcome of your trades, as well as providing a baseline for improving your future trading tactics. Having a trading plan also helps to maximize returns while minimizing losses by controlling the risks associated with trading.

Losses are more likely when there is no trading strategy because of lack of planning and discipline.

Trading without a strategy also allows emotions to influence your trades, which may lead to risky decisions.

Overview of the top best three profitable trading strategies

Trend Trading

Trend trading is a method that entails detecting and following the current direction of a market trend. Traders strive to profit from continuous price moves in one direction, whether upward (bullish trend) or downward (bearish trend).

This strategy can be used by all types of traders, including scalpers, intraday traders, swing traders, and position traders. We'll go into detail on how this strategy can be used by different kinds of traders.

Trend traders seek to enter positions in the direction of the trend, purchasing during uptrends and selling (or shorting) during downtrends. They frequently employ technical indicators like moving averages, trend-lines, and momentum oscillators to confirm and corroborate trend direction.

Traders often enter positions when they see a strong and established trend, which is often followed by a pullback or retracement inside the trend. They want to ride the trend until they see signs of reversal or weariness, at which point they will abandon the position.

This approach can be used by all types of traders, including scalpers, intraday traders, swing traders, and position traders. We'll go into detail about how it can be used by different kinds of traders.

Breakout Trading

Breakout trading entails taking positions when the price of an asset rises above or falls below a critical level of support or resistance. Breakouts occur when the price moves beyond a specified range or consolidation pattern, indicating the possibility of a new trend emerging.

Breakout traders look to capitalize on the momentum created by the breakout, entering positions early in the new trend to maximize profit possibilities. They frequently employ technical analysis techniques including chart patterns (e.g., triangles, rectangles flag, wedge, etc.) and volume indicators to spot possible breakouts.

Traders actively follow price fluctuations, looking for indicators of a breakout above or below resistance levels. Once a breakthrough is confirmed (usually with greater volume), traders establish positions in the breakout's direction and place stop-loss orders to mitigate risk. They may also employ trailing stop-loss orders to capture further gains as the trend progresses.

This strategy can be used by all types of traders, including scalpers, intraday traders, swing traders, and position traders. We'll go into detail on how this strategy can be used by different kinds of traders.

Range Trading

Range trading, also known as mean reversion trading, is purchasing at the lower and selling at the upper limits of a price range or trading range. Traders seek to profit on the cyclical nature of price movements within a specific range, taking advantage of prices' tendency to revert to the mean.

Range traders look for critical support and resistance levels that define the trading range. They want to enter long positions near support levels and short positions near resistance levels, expecting reversals or bounces within the range.

Price action inside the range is actively monitored by traders, who look for opportunities to buy low and sell high. They may employ oscillators such as the Relative Strength Index (RSI) or Stochastic Oscillator to detect overbought and oversold circumstances inside the range, indicating probable entry or exit positions.

This strategy can be used by all types of traders, including scalpers, intraday traders, swing traders, and position traders.

We'll go into detail on how this strategy can be used by different kinds of traders.

Now, let's look into these tactics in detail.

Chapter 2

Strategy 1: (Trend trading strategy)

Trading based on trends is based on the idea that asset prices will continue to move in the same direction as existing trends due to momentum. After determining the direction in which the price of an asset is moving, trend traders initiate positions in that direction.

Trends form when the price of an asset moves regularly in one direction.

This movement might be bullish or bearish, or the price of an asset may move sideways. The longer a trend persists, the more it is regarded "confirmed," and trend traders are more inclined to open a position.

Whether you're a day trader, swing trader, or an investor with a longer time horizon, trend trading can help you increase your chances of success.

Identifying a trend

The most straightforward method for identifying trends is to observe an asset's basic price behavior. Price action (technical) traders believe that the information offered by candlesticks is enough to understand the market.

An uptrend can be identified when the asset's price consistently makes higher highs and higher lows, whereas a downtrend happens when the price makes lower lows and lower highs. The trend is sideways or horizontal when the price oscillates between set levels that serve as support and resistance. Different trends exhibit distinct features in terms of direction, speed, and momentum.

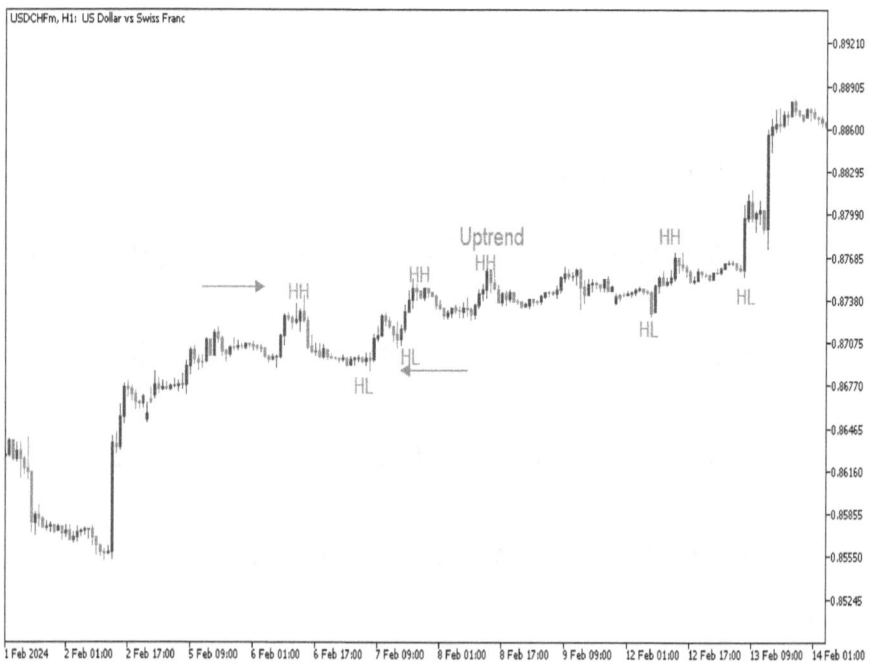

Different types of trends can coexist without contradicting one another. This indicates that trends can exist within trends. There is no single proper trend for any underlying asset until it is assessed in the context of a specific timeline.

A daily chart of an underlying asset may show a growing trend, but when zoomed in to smaller timeframes, such as hourly or 30-minute charts, the trend may appear to be dropping.

Consider a trend as a rising and falling ocean tide. Every tide is composed of smaller waves and ripples. A tide that has been rising for the past hour could be composed of waves and ripples that have fallen in the last few minutes. This is why rising tides ultimately recede and falling tides finally rise. When trading, the period context is critical for identifying and capitalizing on any trend. This is why traders should conduct multi-timeframe analysis.

Obviously, trends on bigger timeframe charts have had a long time to build, and changing direction will require considerably more effort than trends on shorter timeframe charts. Nonetheless, you can always trade the trend based on your timeframe, price targets, and risk appetite.

An upswing can consist of several 'uptrends' or even some 'downtrends'. When utilizing trend-lines, it is critical to consider their gradient or slope. The steeper the slope, the more significant the trend. However, steep trend-lines break more easily than less steep ones. In some circumstances, it is desirable to draw best fit trend-lines rather than recording each swing low or swing high.

Price extremes or spikes might thus be ignored in order to provide a useful price guide in the market. Because trend-lines serve as a guide, it is critical to always look for confluences with other price action indications.

Candlestick and line chart patterns are two of the most effective price movement signals that compliment trend-lines.

Chart patterns help traders understand the raw price action in the market. They essentially assist traders in tracking demand and supply factors in the market using price and time.

Chart patterns reveal three key signals: trend continuation, trend reversal, and trend neutrality.

Important principle and component of trend trading strategy

Trend Confirmation:

Before entering a trade, trend traders frequently seek confirmation from numerous sources to ensure the trend's strength. This could entail studying longer time frames to establish congruence with the overall market direction, or employing numerous technical indicators to corroborate the trend.

Entry and Exit Points.

Setting up effective entry and exit points is critical. Trend traders often look to enter trades in the direction of the trend during pullbacks or retracements, using support and resistance levels as potential entry points in uptrends and downtrends, respectively.

They also create exit points to take profits or cut losses, frequently using support and resistance levels, chart patterns, or technical indicators to determine the best times to enter or exit trades.

Risk Management

Risk management is critical for capital protection. To prevent possible losses, trend traders use risk management tactics like as stop-loss orders, position sizing based on risk tolerance, and following good money management rules.

Support and resistance levels can be used to place stop-loss orders and define risk thresholds for each trade.

Patience and Discipline

To stick to the trading plan and avoid making rash decisions, trend traders must be patient and disciplined. Traders must be prepared to wait for the correct settings rather than chasing every market fluctuation.

Trade management

Once a trade is begun, traders track its progress and alter their strategy accordingly. This could include changing stop-loss orders to lock in profits as the trend develops, or scaling into or out of positions as market conditions change.

Adaptability:

Forex markets are dynamic and can experience abrupt changes in trend direction or volatility. Successful trend traders are adaptive and willing to modify their techniques in response to changing market conditions.

Avoid overtrading.

Stick to your trading strategy and resist the urge to enter transactions based on emotion or impulse. Only trade when your predefined criteria are met, rather than chasing every market change.

Continuous Learning:

Forex trend trading, like any other trading method, demands ongoing study and growth. Traders stay up to date on economic developments, central bank policy, and other factors that can influence currency movements. They also evaluate their trades to identify areas for improvement and refine their strategy over time.

Type of Trend Following Strategies

- Short-term Trend Following Strategy
- Long-term trends based on strategy

Short-term Trend Following Strategy

Trend traders might employ tactics that focus on short- or long-term trends. Short-term traders, such as day traders, will focus on short periods of time and identifiable trends throughout the day in order to profit from short-term price movements. Traders can employ scalping or intraday trend following tactics to capture short-term trends.

Intraday Trend Trading

For traders looking for short-term trends, intraday trend trading is beneficial since they can hold positions until the end of the day. They may analyze trends that are active throughout the day, whether for a few minutes or hours. For example, in an uptrend, a trader might set a trailing stop before the low and again at the next higher low in case of a reversal. If they are following a decline, the trader may employ a short selling approach.

Long-term trend following strategy.

Long-term trend traders typically hold a position for several weeks, months, or even years. Long-term traders utilize fundamental analysis to focus on the long-term trend and the elements that may influence it.

Position trading

Long-term traders typically engage in position trading, which is buying and holding a position for an extended period of time. The focus is on the long-term objective rather than shorter-term trend fluctuations.

Position traders frequently use fundamental research to evaluate probable market price patterns.

Popular trend trading indicators

When developing a trend trading strategy, traders can use technical indicators on trading charts to assist detect trends.

Moving Average Convergence Divergence (MACD)

MACD is an oscillating indicator that can assist traders detect new trends and evaluate whether they are bullish or bearish.

The Relative Strength Index (RSI): is an indicator that helps determine a market's future direction and confirms whether momentum is accelerating or decelerating. They can also determine whether an item was overbought or oversold.

Parabolic SAR: This "stop and reversal system" indicator assists traders in determining the current trend direction and detecting future reversals.

Chapter 3

Strategy 2: (Breakout trading strategy)

Breakout in Trading

A breakout is defined as any price movement that occurs outside of a clearly defined support or resistance level. The breakout might occur at a horizontal or diagonal level, depending on the price action pattern.

Support

Support is a level on a market's chart from which it bounces during a bear trend. Assume an asset is falling but will not fall any lower than a certain price. Every time it reaches that price, buyers take over, and the market rises again. This would be the support level.

When an item reaches a level of support, sellers are unable to reduce its price any further. Buyers may feel that now is the appropriate time to step in, resulting in a reversal.

Support levels will not only arise in bear markets, however. As a bull market zigzags upward, it may eventually reach greater support levels.

You can find support zones on charts of any timeframe. They are occasionally referred to as a base or a floor.

Resistance

Resistance is a point on a market's chart where it has difficulty breaking through to new highs. Resistance is the reverse of support. When an asset hits it, sellers take over and drive its price back down.

Resistance levels, like support levels, can arise during both bear and bull market movements. They are sometimes referred to as the asset's ceiling.

Types of Breakout Strategy

In general, a price action breakout approach can be utilized to join an already established trend or to exit a trend that is likely to reverse fully.

- Continuation breakout strategy and
- Reversal breakout strategy

Continuation Breakout Strategy

As the name implies, the continuation breakout method allows traders to get into an already established trend.

Below are the step-by-step tactics you should use when trading continuation breakouts.

Step 1: Identify an existing trend.

Step 2: Make sure there is a tight consolidation at the end of the impulsive movement.

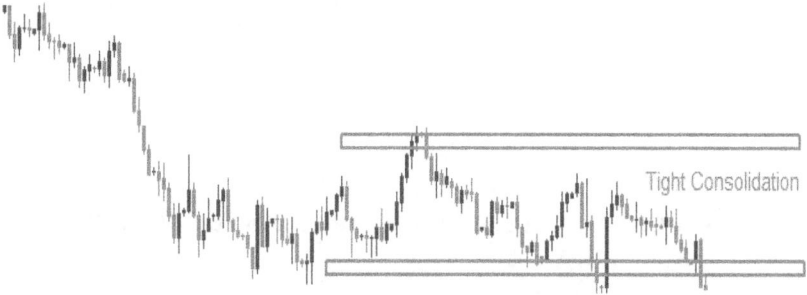

Step 3: Wait for the price to break out of the tight consolidation and produce a continuation candlestick pattern. In this scenario bearish engulfing candlestick.

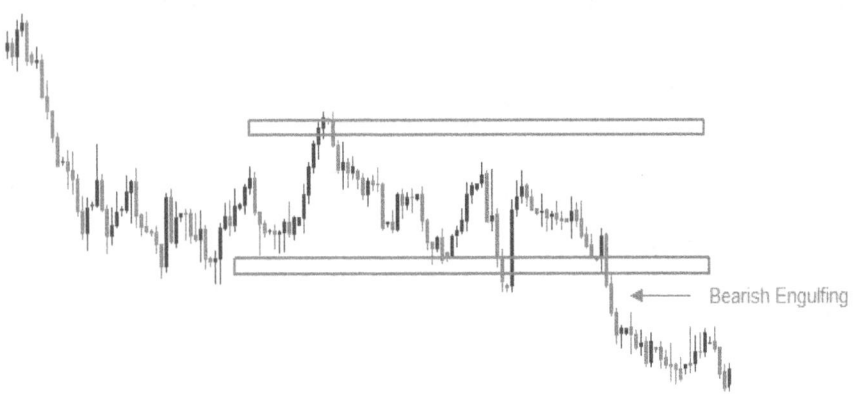

Step 4: You can then place your trade at the break and retest of the support or resistance depending on where the market break out from.

Set your stop loss below the tight consolidation's support when entering a long position and above the tight consolidation's resistance when taking a short position.

Reversal Breakout Strategy

Traders utilize the Reversal Breakout Strategy when a trend that has already ended consolidates for a while before breaking out in the opposite direction.

How to Spot a Reversal Breakout Strategy:

Consider these three factors carefully if you want to know how to spot a reversal breakout:

The price must be at a very strong support or resistance level (particularly on longer timeframes like monthly, weekly, or even daily).

The pricing must have been within a certain range for quite some time.

There must be a candlestick pattern indicating a breakout in the other direction, such as engulfing candles or three white soldiers etc

With these three considerations, it shouldn't be hard to see a reverse breakout.

The following is a step-by-step technique to trading reversal breakouts:

Step 1: Use the three elements described above to determine the end of an existing trend.

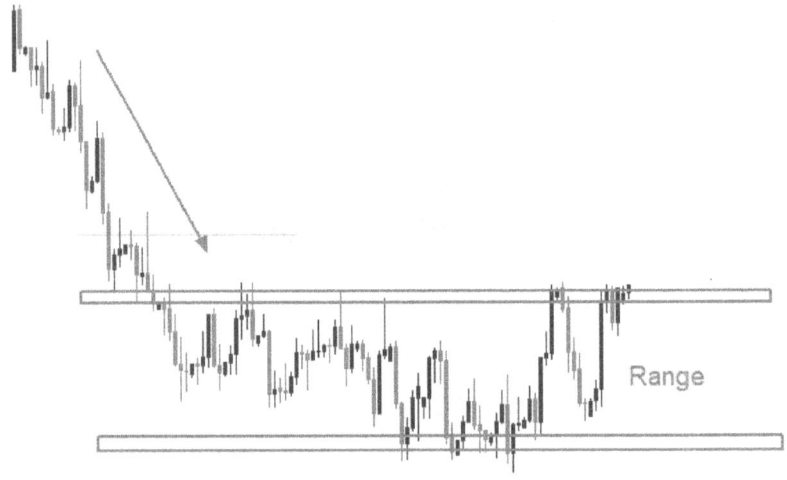

Step 2: Watch for a breakout from the consolidation or range. For example, consider the bullish engulfing candle in the diagram below.

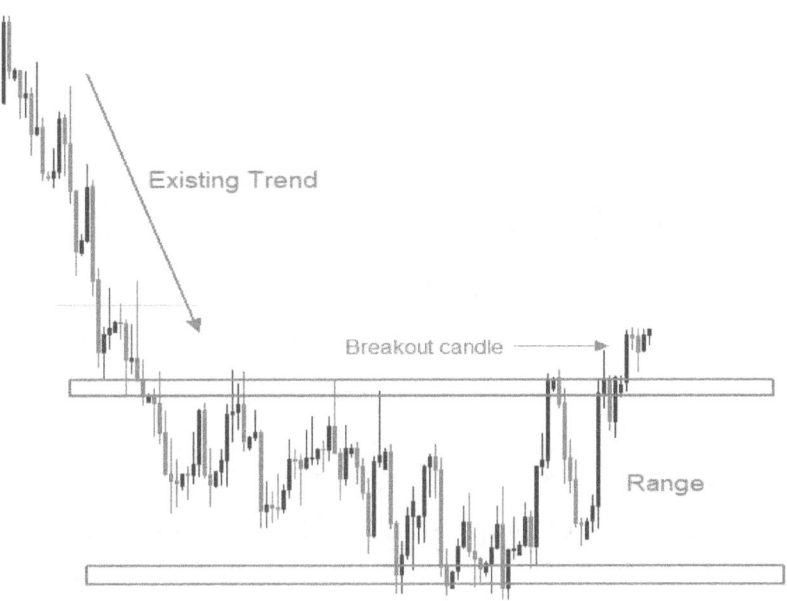

Step 3: Set your stop loss below or above the support or resistance levels. The take profit can be set as strategically as you like.

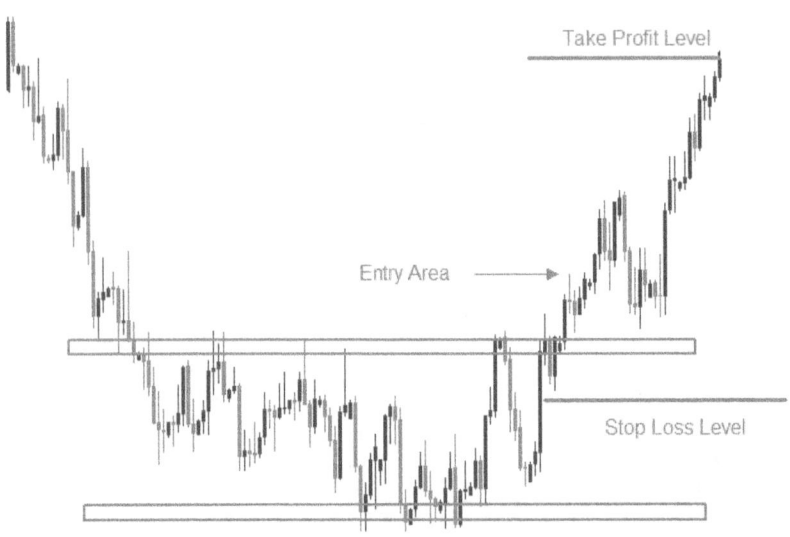

If you follow the principles outlined above, adopting these breakout tactics will boost your chances of making a winning trade.

However, not all breakouts are certain to occur. After all, the market simply uses historical prices to predict future price fluctuations.

Sometimes you observe price breaks below the support or above the resistance line giving you breakout signs but reverse back into the range. This breakout technique is known as false breakouts or fake-out.

False Breakouts

A fake breakout is a reversal price movement, sometimes known as market manipulation, in which the price breaks below or above the zone before swiftly and impulsively reversing. It can occur in either resistance or support zones.

Unfortunately, many inexperienced traders are frequent victims of this trap.

When the price breaks through a support or resistance zone, inexperienced traders see it as a wonderful opportunity to enter a trade.

How to Trade a False Breakout

Step 1: Identify strong bullish/bearish candles at resistance/support levels, excluding previous highs and lows.

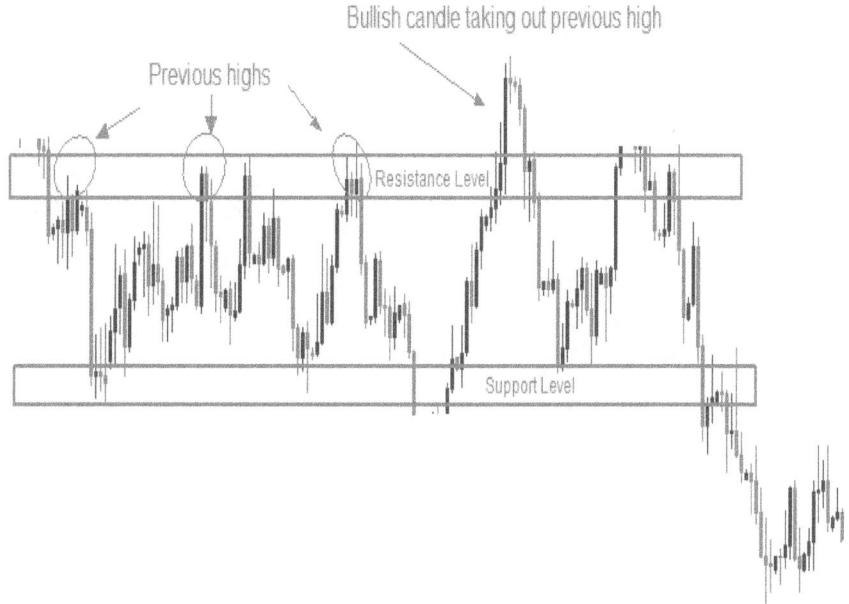

Step 2: Wait for a big body reversal candlestick.

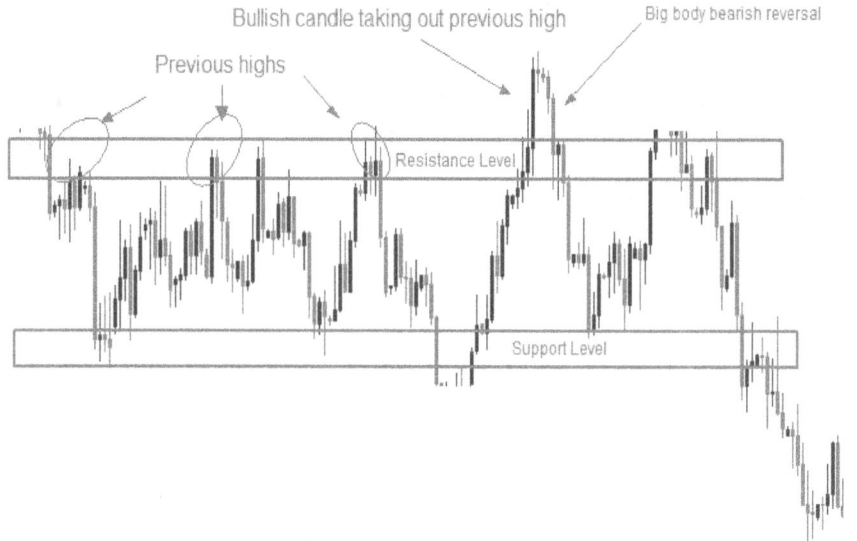

Step 3: Look for a very strategic and logic area to place your entry, it is safer to wait for a break and a retest of either the support level or the resistance level depending or where the market break out from before entry a trade.

In the case of the diagram below the market broke to the down side and retested the support level.

When considering stop loss placement, use a very local area, just like the one in the diagram below, your stop loss should not be too tight to avoid being stop out easily or too wide to avoid huge losses if the market goes against you, but incase if you want to use a wide stop, then you have to reduce your lot size for proper risk management.

Chapter 4

Strategy 3: (Range or a sideways trading strategy)

A sideways market occurs when prices oscillate in a narrow range for an extended length of time without moving in either direction.

In a sideways market, the price varies horizontally rather than vertically. It indicates that neither the bulls (buyers) nor the bears (sellers) are in charge.

A sideways market is defined as an area of support and resistance where prices move. It is also known as non-trending, range-bound, or choppy markets.

In a range market you buy at support, take profit at resistance, and sell at resistance take profit at support level; just as illustrated in the diagram above.

Identifying a Range or Sideways Market

To find a sideways market, first identify support and resistance levels.

When a price rises and then falls, resistance is the highest point before the drop. The resistance level represents an excess of sellers. In contrast, when the price rises again, the low point attained prior to the rise serves as support, support level denotes an excess of buyers.

Trading sideways requires you to look for a price pattern within these levels, price move above and below the resistance and support level, but fails to break a higher high or lower low.

If the price rises above the resistance level and breaks the higher high, it indicates that the sideways trend is going to finish. However, if the price falls below the support level, shattering the lower low, the sideways market would finish.

How do you know when a range or sideways market will end

It is impossible to predict when a sideways market will end because the price can break higher highs or lower lows or continue moving as before.

One way to answer this question is to check the news. If there is significant news coming up, such as the Federal Reserve Policy statement, there is a potential that a breakout will occur and a sideways market may end. You can also use a volume indicator, MFI (Money Flow Index), to determine the volume. If volume is substantial, the sideways market will likely terminate.

Advantages of trading a range or sideways market

Here are the two primary advantages:

- A sideways market has distinct exit and entry points due to the presence of support and resistance levels. These levels represent the highest and lowest price levels, allowing you to pinpoint exit and entry points.

- Sideways trading does not last long in low time periods. This indicates that a sideways market can last for a few days or a week longer. As a result, you can close your trades before a major news announcement or unforeseen incident.

Limitations of trading a range or sideways market

Here are the two primary limitations:

In a sideways market, everything moves quickly, and the number of deals increases significantly. This means it takes more time than other trading strategy. You must monitor your positions throughout the day.

Trading sideways creates more trading opportunities, and traders want to enter every time. This continuous buying and selling has a hefty cost.

Chapter 5

Conclusion

Before we conclude, it is critical that we understand the following points because it influences our trading decisions.

Time frame

Choosing a time frame that fits your trading strategy is critical. For a trader, there is a significant difference between trading on a 15-minute chart and a weekly chart.

If you want to be a scalper, a trader who profits from tiny market movements, you should focus on lower time frames, such as 1-minute to 15-minute charts.

Swing traders, on the other hand, are more likely to generate profitable trading chances by using both a 4-hour and a daily chart. As a result, before deciding on your chosen trading technique, consider how long you want to stay in a transaction.

Position size

It is critical to determine the optimal trading size. Successful trading methods require you to understand your risk tolerance.

Excessive risk-taking might result in significant losses.

A typical piece of advice in this regard is to set a risk limit for each deal. For example, traders frequently set a 1% limit on their trades, which means they will not risk more than 1% of their account on a single transaction.

Create a sound trading plan

Before you begin trading, you should have a clear trading plan that outlines your objectives, risk tolerance, and trading techniques. This plan should be tailored to your specific circumstances, taking into account things like your financial condition, time horizon, and investing goals.

With a sound trading plan, you will be able to make informed decision while avoiding emotional trading. When you develop a plan, be disciplined enough to stick to it regardless of what the market does.

Practice with a demo account

Practice makes perfect, especially when it comes to trading. Before you start trading with real money, it's best to practice on a demo account. A demo account enables you to trade with virtual money and test your methods in a risk-free environment.

This will give you more confidence and experience before you begin trading with real money.

Choose the Right Broker

Choosing the correct broker is critical for success in Forex trading. You want to work with a broker who is honest, trustworthy, and has a solid market reputation. Look for a broker that has cheap spreads, quick execution, and a simple trading platform. It's also crucial to confirm that the broker is regulated by a respectable regulatory agency.

Continuously educate yourself

Learning is an ongoing process, which is especially true when it comes to trading because the industry is continuously evolving, it's critical to keep up with the latest news, trends, and strategies. This can be accomplished through reading books, attending webinars, and following skilled traders on social media channels. By continuing to educate yourself, you will be able to make sounds decisions and respond to market developments.

Thank you for purchasing this book, the next page contains the link to the free video bonus package

Video access link

https://www.youtube.com/playlist?list=PLsr29W8GhQK1kTxsZ-FzvxMt80z7yA-lv

Link to Other Video Course

subscribepage.io/freeforexcourse

www.ingramcontent.com/pod-product-compliance
Lightning Source LLC
Chambersburg PA
CBHW070407230526
45471CB00006B/2694